The "Reason Why" Books

COAL
REVISED EDITION

Irving and Ruth Adler

The John Day Company   New York
an Intext publisher

THE "REASON WHY" BOOKS

Revised Edition
Copyright © 1974 by Irving Adler
Copyright © 1965 by Irving Adler and Ruth Adler

Library of Congress Cataloging in Publication Data
Adler, Irving.
    Coal.
    (Their The "reason why" books)
    SUMMARY: A history and survey of coal and coal mining, from its formation in the earth to its use as fuel.
    Includes bibliographical references.
    1. Coal—Juvenile literature. [1. Coal]
I. Adler, Ruth, joint author. II. Title.
TN801.A3 1974   553'.2   74-5304
ISBN 0-381-99974-2 GB

First edition published 1965—five impressions
Revised edition published 1974

The John Day Company, 257 Park Avenue South, New York, N.Y. 10010.

Published on the same day in Canada by Longman Canada Limited.

Printed in the United States of America.

Contents

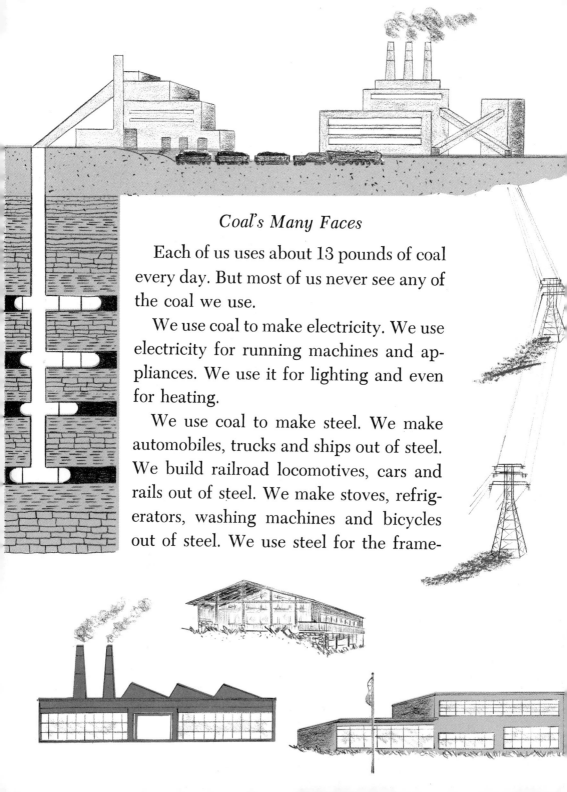

Coal's Many Faces

Each of us uses about 13 pounds of coal every day. But most of us never see any of the coal we use.

We use coal to make electricity. We use electricity for running machines and appliances. We use it for lighting and even for heating.

We use coal to make steel. We make automobiles, trucks and ships out of steel. We build railroad locomotives, cars and rails out of steel. We make stoves, refrigerators, washing machines and bicycles out of steel. We use steel for the frame-

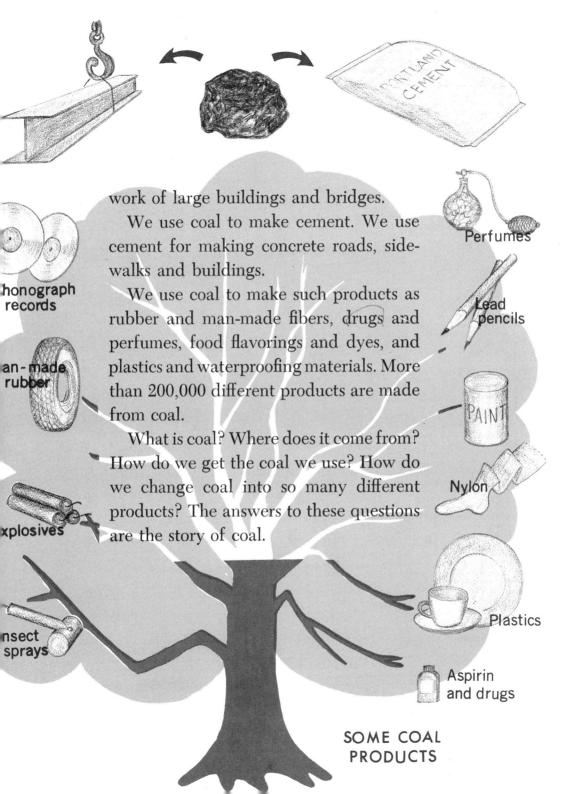

work of large buildings and bridges.

We use coal to make cement. We use cement for making concrete roads, sidewalks and buildings.

We use coal to make such products as rubber and man-made fibers, drugs and perfumes, food flavorings and dyes, and plastics and waterproofing materials. More than 200,000 different products are made from coal.

What is coal? Where does it come from? How do we get the coal we use? How do we change coal into so many different products? The answers to these questions are the story of coal.

Phonograph records

Man-made rubber

Explosives

Insect sprays

Perfumes

Lead pencils

PAINT

Nylon

Plastics

Aspirin and drugs

SOME COAL
PRODUCTS

A leaf fossil found in a coal mine

Coal: The Fossil That We Burn

Coal is found in *beds* or *seams* in the earth's crust. The coal beds are separated from each other by layers of *shale* or *sandstone*. Shale and sandstone are *sedimentary* (SED-uh-MEN-tuh-ree) rocks that were formed at the bottoms of seas and oceans millions of years ago. In some places there are more than 100 different coal seams, one above the other. All the seams together are called *coal measures*. Coal measures are sometimes many thousands of feet thick. *Fossil* (FOS-suhl) plants are often found in coal and in the rocks right next to the coal beds. Fossils are remains of plants and animals that lived millions of years ago. Whole fossil tree stumps are sometimes found in coal beds. The stumps have their fossil roots in the rocks next to the coal beds.

The sedimentary rocks that separate coal seams and

the plant fossils that have been found in these rocks and in coal are clues that helped geologists discover how coal was formed. Geologists were helped, too, by looking at coal under a microscope. What they saw looked a lot the way wood looks under a microscope. The clues made geologists decide that coal was formed from woody plants.

Coal was formed from great fern-like trees and other plants that grew in large swamps along the shallow seas that covered the earth's surface about 300 million years ago. The plants grew quickly to their great size because the climate was very warm and there was lots of rainfall. When the plants died, they fell into the swamps where they were covered by mud. They did not rot completely, the way dead plants do on dry land, because air could not reach them. Instead they changed slowly into a slimy material called *peat*. Peat is usually brown, moist and spongy and contains many plant remains.

New plants kept growing, dying and partly rotting in the swamps. This went on for a long time, forming layers of peat hundreds of feet thick. Then the sea moved in over the swamps and covered the peat with water. Rivers flowed into the sea, carrying mud and sand. The mud and sand fell to the bottom of the sea and buried the peat. The weight of the water, mud and sand, pressing down on the peat, squeezed the juices out of the peat and changed it to *lignite* (LIG-nite). Lignite is a brown-ish black coal that crumbles easily. It contains many plant remains, too. The mud and sand were pressed together, too, and were changed into sedimentary rocks. The mud became shale and the sand became sandstone.

Later the land rose up, pushing the sea back. New swamps formed along the edge of the sea, where the old swamps had been. New plants grew in the swamps. Then the same thing happened all over again. New layers of peat were formed and were buried under new layers of mud and sand. New layers of lignite and rock were formed. Each new layer of lignite was a coal seam. As new layers of lignite and new rocks were formed, the upper layers pressed down hard on the lignite seams, changing them to *bituminous* (by-TYOU-muh-nus) or *soft* coal. Bituminous coal is black and breaks easily. Twenty feet of plant material were pressed together to make one foot of bituminous coal.

In some places on the earth, the rock layers separating coal beds have folded upward forming mountains. In

How coal was formed
Giant fern-like trees...

...died and fell into the swamps and partly rotted.

these places the coal was pressed together with a great force, changing the bituminous coal to *anthracite* (AN-thruh-site) coal. Anthracite coal is black and very hard. There is very little of it. In the United States it is found only in a small area of Pennsylvania.

All living things contain carbon, in addition to hydrogen, oxygen, nitrogen, sulphur and other elements. When plants were changed into coal, much of the oxygen and hydrogen was squeezed out of them, leaving mostly pure carbon. Lignite, which was squeezed the least, has the smallest amount of pure carbon in it. Anthracite coal is almost all pure carbon. So lignite has the lowest *rank* in the coal family and anthracite coal has the highest rank.

In addition to carbon, coal contains other elements that were in the plants from which it was formed. So coal is made up mostly of carbon with smaller amounts of hydrogen, oxygen, nitrogen, sulphur and *mineral ash*. The mineral ash is made up of small amounts of more than 30 other different elements.

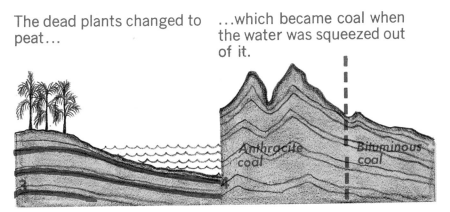

The dead plants changed to peat...

...which became coal when the water was squeezed out of it.

Anthracite coal

Bituminous coal

Coal's Early History

Marco Polo was an Italian who lived about 700 years ago. In 1271 he went to China on a trading expedition. He returned to Italy 25 years later with many tales of the strange and wonderful things he saw in China. He told about the "black stones" that the Chinese people were burning as a fuel. The "black stones" were coal. The Chinese had been digging and using coal for more than two thousand years.

Coal was hardly known in Italy during Marco Polo's time. However, some coal had been dug and used in England since the 9th century. This coal was dug from coal seams that were on the surface of the ground.

In England coal was first used as a fuel where high temperatures were needed. Coal was used as a fuel by the early lime-burners who needed high temperatures to make lime. They made lime by heating limestone or sea-shells in great kilns. Coal was used as a fuel by smiths who needed high temperatures to work and shape iron into useful products. Iron was heated in the burning coals of a forge until it was red or white hot. Then the iron became soft enough to be worked and shaped.

Coal was used as a fuel where large amounts of liquid had to be heated. It was used by brewers and dyers. It was used for heating water for washing clothes.

The lime burners of 350 years ago used coal as a fuel in their lime-kilns.

Coal was used as a fuel in fireplaces for heating homes. It was used as a fuel for baking bricks.

By the end of the 17th century large amounts of coal were being burned in London. The coal smoke that poured out of the chimneys of homes and workshops hung over the city in a thick black cloud. One British writer of that time said the black clouds over London looked like the clouds over a volcano.

More Coal and New Problems

At the beginning of the seventeenth century wood was becoming scarce in England. Because it was becoming scarce it was becoming too costly to use as a fuel. This increased the demand for coal.

The best coal mines in Europe at this time were along the Tyne River in northern England, where there were coal seams on the surface of the ground. It was easier to dig coal from these surface out-croppings than from seams elsewhere that were many feet below ground. Coal from along the Tyne could be carried easily by ships to distant places because there was an excellent seaport, Newcastle-on-Tyne, right near the coal mines. Because Newcastle coal was easier to mine and easier to transport, it was cheaper than coal mined elsewhere in Europe. Coal from Newcastle was even carried across the English Channel to the seaports of France. Because Newcastle coal was transported by sea, it came to be known as "sea coal." And because coal was so plentiful in Newcastle, an expression arose that we still use. We say it is "like carrying coals to Newcastle" if we give someone something that he already has a lot of.

As coal in the surface out-croppings was used up, shafts had to be dug through the rock between the coal seams to reach coal in the lower seams. And as coal mines became deeper, new problems began to develop. Water seeped through the ground into the mines, flooding them. The problem of draining out the water was not solved easily. Pumps, operated by people or animals, pumped water out of the mines. As mines got deeper, however, hundreds of horses had to be used to keep the mines free of water. This became very costly. The drainage problem was finally solved when the steam engine was invented and steam engines took over the work that had been done by horses.*

Rag-and-chain pump used about 400 years ago for draining water from mines.

* For more information about steam engines see *Machines,* by the same authors, The John Day Company, 1964.

In dyeing, the fire and the dye were in separate containers.

Coal Changes Industry

With coal being used more and more in industry, more problems developed. The change to coal as a fuel from wood or charcoal was very easy where the fire and the things being heated by the fire were in separate containers. That is why coal was first used successfully by dyers, salt makers, brewers and lime-burners.

Coal could not be used successfully at first for glass-making because the glass-blowers had to heat the glass right in the burning fuel. The fumes of burning coal made the glass-blowers sick. In England, however, a law was passed in 1621 saying that the glass-makers could no longer use wood as a fuel. As a result, coal-fired furnaces were invented for use in glass-making. Using this kind of furnace, sheet-glass for window panes could be made cheaply. Glass-blowing could not be done in England again until a different furnace was invented that protected the glass blower from the coal fumes.

Coal could not be used successfully at first for iron-making either. Iron was made by heating iron ore and charcoal together in a furnace. When coal was used in place of charcoal, the iron turned out to be brittle. The use of coal became practical after 1784 when a method was invented for changing this brittle iron into a soft iron that could be shaped and worked. We shall read about this on page 33.

In glass blowing, the glass was put right into the fire.

Mining in the 18th and Early 19th Centuries

The steam engine made it possible to pump water out of mines by machine. The steam engine, however, was large and clumsy and could only be used at the surface. To work the mine pumps, its power had to be applied through a series of straight iron rods that passed down the mine shaft. So the steam engine could not be used to operate a coal cutting machine. Cutting coal continued to be done by hand until the end of the 19th century when new sources of power and cheap ways of making strong steel were developed.

A miner cut coal by hand with the help of a hand pick and a crowbar. He worked kneeling down or lying on his side. With his pick and crowbar he *undercut* the coal by making a deep groove near the bottom of the *face* of the coal seam. If the coal was soft, he could then loosen it with the help of a wedge or a crowbar. If the coal was hard, the miner used a drill to make holes in the coal face. He put gunpowder into the holes and then exploded the gunpowder. The explosion loosened the coal above the groove.

For many years the coal was hauled out of the mine by hand too. Underground passageways led from the mine shaft to the working faces. The coal was hauled along these passageways in wicker baskets that had been placed on wooden sleds. Men or women dragged the sleds along the ground. Sometimes ponies pulled the sleds.

Towards the end of the 18th century carts with wheels took the place of the wooden sleds. Young boys called *trolly boys* pulled the coal-filled carts from the coal face to the mine shaft.

Removing the coal from the mine was often back-breaking work. At first women or boys carried the coal on their backs in wicker baskets. They had to climb steep ladders or steps that had been built inside the mine shaft. Later, machines operated by horses were used for hauling out the coal. After the steam engine was invented and improved, steam power was used for hauling.

Women carried the coal in baskets up steep steps inside the mine shaft.

Removing coal from the mine

When the coal seams near the Tyne were used up, coal began to be mined at great distances from seaports. This meant that the coal had to be carried overland to the seaports, where it was loaded onto ships. To help keep the cost of coal down, inclined railways were built. Wooden rails were laid on the ground. The rails sloped downhill from the mines to the docks along the rivers. Gravity pulled loaded coal wagons downhill over the rails. Horses trotted behind the loaded wagons. When the wagons were unloaded at the docks, the horses pulled the empty wagons uphill again to the mines. These coal-wagon railways were the earliest ancestors of the railroad.

Danger in the Mine

Drainage was not the only problem of underground mines. Poison gases that formed in the mines made a miner's work dangerous. Underground explosions made a miner's work dangerous, too.

Miners carried candles to light their way as they worked. A miner sometimes found that his candle flame grew dimmer and dimmer. At the same time he found it harder and harder to breathe. This happened because the miner had come upon a pocket of gas that had little oxygen in it and was mostly carbon dioxide. Flames cannot burn without oxygen. Animals cannot stay alive without oxygen to breathe. The miners called this gas *blackdamp* or *chokedamp*. The word *damp* comes from the German word *Dampf* which means vapor.

As deeper mines were dug, underground explosions often occurred. Hundreds of miners were killed in mine explosions. The explosions had two causes. *Methane* (MEH-thane) gas was one cause of underground explosions. When plants changed to coal, millions of years ago, methane gas was given off. The methane gas collected in pockets in the coal seams. Sometimes, when the coal was mined, the pockets were opened up and the methane gas escaped into the mine where it mixed with air. If the methane mixed with just the right amount of air, it formed a mixture that could explode. The miner's candle made the mixture explode like a bomb. The miners called this explosive mixture *firedamp.* Fine coal dust that collected underground during mining was another cause of mine explosions. When coal dust is mixed with just the right amount of air, an explosive mixture is formed, too.

Carbon monoxide gas, which is a deadly poison, is formed after mine fires or explosions. Carbon monoxide has no taste or smell and the miners had no way of detecting it until it was too late. They called carbon monoxide gas *afterdamp* because it appeared after fires and explosions.

A fireman, wrapped in wet sackcloth, burning firedamp at the working face

Early Attempts to Make Mines Safe

At first almost nothing was done to get rid of choke-damp. If a miner found that his candle flame was growing dimmer, he knew that there was chokedamp in the place where he was digging coal. So he moved to a part of the mine where the air was fresher. He could tell that the air was fresher because his candle burned brightly once more.

Getting rid of firedamp was the job of a "fireman." The fireman was a very brave miner who had the job of burning the firedamp before it could explode. The fireman wrapped himself from head to foot in wet sackcloth. He crawled along the floor of the mine carrying a lighted candle that was fastened to the end of a long stick. He held the candle close to the ground until he came to the working face. Then he covered his head with wet sackcloth and reached toward the working face with the lighted candle. Any firedamp near the face would burn. Then the working face was believed to be safe.

Mines still were not safe, however. More and more miners died each year in explosions. *Ventilating* (VEN-tih-LATE-ing) the mines helped solve the problem of mine explosions. Passageways were dug for bringing in fresh air and taking out bad air. Air pumps made the air move along the passageways.

The invention of the safety lamp helped solve the

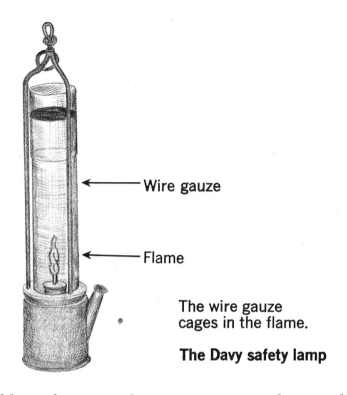

Wire gauze

Flame

The wire gauze cages in the flame.

The Davy safety lamp

problem of mine explosions, too. It was known that the miners' candles caused the firedamp to explode. So miners stopped carrying candles and began to carry decaying fish. Rotting fish gave off light like the light of fireflies. But the light wasn't bright enough for the miners to work by. And the smell of the fish was very unpleasant. In 1815 the great English scientist, Sir Humphrey Davy, was asked to make a miner's lamp that would be safe to use in the mines. Within three months he invented such a lamp. The Davy lamp had a wire screen around the flame of the lamp. The flame could not pass through the wire screen. So the flame was caged in and could not cause explosions.

Mining Today: Underground Mining and Surface Mining

The pictures on page 24 show different kinds of modern coal mines. *Surface mining* is done where the coal seams lie close to the surface. Surface mining is also called *strip* or *open-pit* mining. *Shaft mines, drift mines* and *slope mines* are different kinds of *underground mines.* In the United States, 3 out of 5 coal mines are underground, but they produce only half of the coal.

Most coal in the United States is now mined by machine. In surface mining, huge mining shovels, powered by electricity, scoop up great bites of earth and rock, uncovering the coal seams. Some mining shovels are taller than a 20 story building. After the coal seams have been uncovered, machines that work like mechanical street sweepers sweep the coal seam clean. Then smaller power shovels scoop up the coal and dump it into huge trucks. The trucks carry the coal to a *preparation plant* where the coal is cleaned and sorted according to size.

In some places where surface mining is done the coal seams extend under hilly land. In these places the coal is loosened by huge drills that drill straight into the side of the hill. The drills, called *augers* (AW-gurrs), are sometimes 7 feet across. They can drill 200 feet into a hillside. The coal comes out along the spiral turns of the auger. In places where auger mining can be done, the "Push-

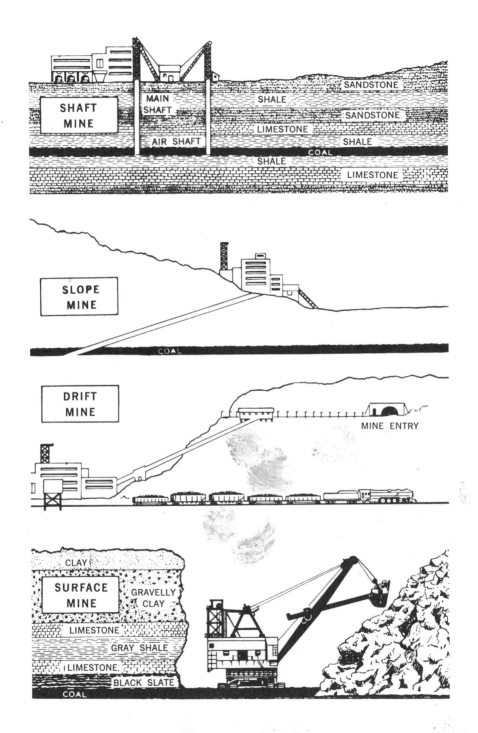

SHAFT MINE
MAIN SHAFT
AIR SHAFT
SANDSTONE
SHALE
SANDSTONE
LIMESTONE
SHALE
COAL
SHALE
LIMESTONE

SLOPE MINE
COAL

DRIFT MINE
MINE ENTRY

SURFACE MINE
CLAY
GRAVELLY CLAY
LIMESTONE
GRAY SHALE
LIMESTONE
BLACK SLATE
COAL

button Miner" can be used, too. The Pushbutton Miner is operated by only one man. It is completely automatic. As it scoops out the coal, it dumps the coal into carrying cars that are stored, until they are needed, on a spiral ramp of the Pushbutton Miner.

After the coal in a surface mine has been mined-out, the soil that had been scooped up by the huge mining shovels should be put back. Trees and grass should be planted to keep the soil from being washed away by rain and melting snow and to keep it from being blown away by the wind. This has been done in some places. Where it has not been done, floods occur causing great damage.

Coal is cut in the three kinds of underground mines in the same way. In most underground mines the under-cutting is done by electrically-powered cutting machines that look like giant chain saws. Then the coal is loosened by blasting. The blasting is done mechanically, too. When the coal in the face is blasted loose, miners say it is "blown down." Loading machines scoop up the loosened coal. They dump the coal onto a moving belt or into a wait-ing *shuttle* car which starts it on its trip out of the mine. In a shaft mine, the moving belts or shuttle cars carry the coal to the base of the shaft. Elevators then lift the coal out of the mine. In a drift mine, the moving belts or shuttle cars carry the coal straight out to the mine entrance in the side of the hill. In a slope mine, the coal

The largest power shovel in the world

Auger mining

The Pushbutton Miner

A preparation plant

A coal cutter

A driller

A shuttle car

A continuous miner

is carried out of the mine by moving belts or electric railways that travel from the coal seams, along the sloping tunnel, to the surface. At the surface, the coal is prepared for use in a preparation plant.

Since 1951 more and more underground mining is being done by a machine called the *continuous miner*. A continuous miner cuts, loads and even hauls the coal out of the mine in one continuous operation. No blasting has to be done when a continuous miner is used. Continuous miners now cut more than half the coal that is mined underground. A miner who operates a continuous miner can mine as much as eight tons of coal in a minute. Miners who work underground still do not mine more than 14 tons of coal a day. This is because underground coal seams are so hard to get at. A miner who works in a strip mine produces about 36 tons of coal in a day. This is because the coal seams are easy to reach with huge mining machines.

Miners who work in underground mines go to the working faces along the same passageways through which the coal is taken out. In a shaft mine, the miners go down to the working level of the mine in an elevator in the mine shaft. They are then carried to the working face in a train of *man-trip cars* pulled by an electric locomotive. In slope and drift mines, the miners get into the man-trip cars right at the mine entrance.

Miners entering a train of man-trip cars

Underground Mining Methods

Underground mines are worked either by the *room and pillar* method or the *longwall* method.

In room and pillar mining a network of tunnels, somewhat like a network of city streets, is cut into the coal seam. The ceiling of a tunnel is called its *roof*. The tunnels are separated from each other by large pillars of coal. Each pillar becomes a working face from which coal is cut. The tunnels are used for hauling coal away from the face. They are also used for ventilation. As more and more coal is cut, the pillars become smaller and smaller and the tunnels become bigger and bigger until they are more like rooms than tunnels. Finally the rooms are so big and the pillars are so small that it is no longer safe to cut any more coal from the pillars. At this point, the roofs are made to cave in and mining is moved to another seam. The roofs are made to cave in to prevent accidental and dangerous cave-ins later.

In longwall mining, a long working face is cut, starting at the base of the mine shaft. Coal is then cut from this working face. As more and more coal is cut, the working face moves farther and farther back from the shaft. The mined out places are not allowed to become rooms, however. As soon as a place is mined out, it is filled up with rocks and dirt. Passageways are kept open for hauling coal and for ventilation.

Most mines in the United States use the room and pillar method. It can be used where mines are not very deep and where the coal seams are straight. Then there is little danger of roof cave-ins as the pillars are being cut away. Pillar mining takes less work than longwall mining, but less coal can be taken out.

In many places in Europe where mines are very deep and the coal seams dip down sharply, the roofs of mined out areas are not strong enough for the pillar method to be used. So most European mines use longwall mining. More and more longwall mining is being done now in the United States because new mining machines have been built that speed up longwall mining.

Safety in the Mines

Coal mining is dangerous work. But mines are less dangerous now than they used to be. In 1930 about 70,000 coal miners were injured in the United States, and about 1600 were killed by accidents in the mines. Now about 10,000 coal miners are injured each year, and an average of 240 are killed by accidents each year. Mines are not completely safe, but they are safer than they used to be because mine operators now know more about the causes of mine accidents. So they know what to do to reduce the number of accidents. They are safer, too, because of the efforts of the miners, through their unions, and of other concerned people. As a result of these efforts, most governments now have safety rules that the mine operators must follow.

In the United States, safety rules are made both by the states and by the Bureau of Mines of the United States

A "safety man" testing for methane gas. Like all miners, he wears a hard hat equipped with an electric safety lamp.

Department of Interior. The Bureau of Mines publishes books and articles to teach mine officials how to prevent mine accidents. It explains how to test for methane gas and describes the best ventilating methods. It explains how coal dust explosions can be prevented by *rock-dusting* mine walls with a coating of powdered limestone. It explains how to prevent roof cave-ins in underground mines. The Bureau of Mines tests mine equipment and then approves the equipment that has passed its tests.

The Bureau of Mines has a crew of mine inspectors. They inspect the mines to make sure that safety rules are being followed and to see that only permissible equipment is being used.

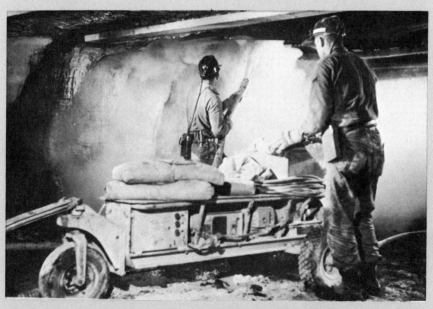

Rock-dusting mine walls helps prevent mine explosions.

Some Important Coal Customers

Less than one ton out of every twenty-five tons of coal mined in the United States is anthracite coal. Most of the coal being mined is bituminous coal.

Anthracite coal is used chiefly for heating homes. It makes almost no smoke when it burns. Its hardness makes it cleaner and easier to store and handle.

Some bituminous coal is used for heating, too. It is used for heating large buildings, such as schools, hospitals and factories. Completely automatic coal furnaces, fed by moving underground belts, can make bituminous coal heating clean and efficient.

Three-fifths of the bituminous coal that is mined is used for making electricity. Coal is used to heat great quantities of water to produce the steam that powers steam turbines. More than half the electricity we use is made by steam turbines at power plants that use coal as a fuel.

The steel industry is coal's second best customer. American steel companies use about one-sixth of the bituminous coal mined in the United States. An additional one-tenth is sent abroad to steel companies in France, Germany, Italy and Japan. The steel industry uses coal to make *coke*. Coke is made by heating coal without air in special ovens called *coking ovens*. Coke takes the place of charcoal in iron-making. Iron-making is the first step in making steel. *

The cement industry also depends on coal as a fuel. Coal is used to heat the kilns in which cement is made. The cement industry uses powdered coal.

Industries that use a lot of coal have their coal delivered to them in *unit trains.* Unit trains of more than 100 cars carry as much as 10,000 tons of coal at passenger train speeds directly from the mine to the consumer. Using unit trains, railroads can charge low rates for carrying coal. Low rates help keep down the cost of bituminous coal.

Some electric companies have kept down the cost of coal by building their power plants right next to coal mines. It is cheaper to carry electricity over wires to distant users than to carry coal from the mine to a distant power plant.

One large coal company delivers coal to a customer by pipeline. The pipeline carries a mixture of water and powdered coal across mountains and desert from the mine to a power plant 275 miles away. The company stopped using the pipeline when railroads lowered their rates for carrying coal. New pipelines, however, are being planned in other places.

* For information on how steel is made, see *Learning About Steel: Through the Story of a Nail,* by the same authors, The John Day Company, 1961.

34

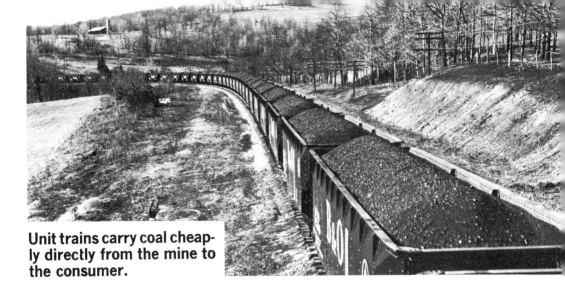

Unit trains carry coal cheaply directly from the mine to the consumer.

Coal's By-products

Before the electric lamp was invented, streets and houses were lighted by gas made from coal. Coal gas was made in special ovens at gasworks by heating coal without any air. Coal gas was also made when coal was heated to make coke. This gas went up the chimneys of the coke ovens and was wasted.

About 100 years ago the English chemist, William Henry Perkin, had the idea that he could use the tars that collected in the chimneys of gasworks and coke ovens to make the medicine, quinine (KWY-nine). Until Perkin's time quinine had been made from the bark of certain trees. Perkin never did succeed in making quinine from coal tar. But, by accident, he did make the first man-made dye, a purple called mauve (MOVH). Perkin's discovery was the beginning of a great new indus-

35

try, the industry of coal by-products.

Since Perkin's time, more than 200,000 different coal by-products have been made. Some by-products are made from coal tar. Other by-products are made from coal gas. Coal tar products include dyes, perfumes, medicines, food flavorings, explosives, vitamins, weed killers, insect killers, and nylon and other plastics. Coal gas products include ammonia, man-made rubber, gasoline, fuel oils, cleaning fluids, fertilizers and some plastics. We usually get gasoline and fuel oil from petroleum. Germany, however, has no oil wells but has large coal deposits. So, during World War II, Germany made all the gasoline it used from coal.

The Chemistry of Coal and Coal By-products

Each coal by-product is a complicated chemical *compound* that has *atoms* of carbon, hydrogen and other chemicals in it. The smallest unit of a compound is a *molecule* (MOLL-uh-kyoul) of that compound. An atom of carbon is the smallest unit of carbon. An atom of hydrogen is the smallest unit of hydrogen, and so on. Atoms and most molecules are so small that we cannot see them even with the help of the most powerful microscopes.

The molecule of each coal by-product has its own special pattern of the way its atoms are joined together. The patterns are of two kinds. The atoms of coal tar chemicals are joined together to form molecules with ring-shaped patterns. The coal tar products belong to the family of *aromatic* (AAR-uh-MAT-ik) compounds. They are called aromatic because of their strong smell or *aroma* (uh-ROW-muh). The atoms of coal gas chemicals are joined together to form molecules with chain-shaped patterns. The coal gas products belong to the family of *aliphatic* (AAL-uh-FAT-ik) compounds. Aliphatic means oily or fatty.

We can see what the ring-shaped and chain-shaped patterns look like if we understand how atoms join themselves to other atoms. Each atom joins itself to other atoms by *bonds.* The bonds are like hands by which the atoms can hold on to each other. Each carbon atom has four bonds by which it can join itself to other atoms. Each hydrogen atom has only one bond by which it can join itself to other atoms.

Since a carbon atom has four bonds and a hydrogen atom has only one bond, a single carbon atom can join itself to four hydrogen atoms. The result is a molecule of methane. Methane is the simplest of the aliphatic compounds. The diagram below shows how a chemist pictures a methane molecule. Each line in the diagram stands for a bond.

$$\text{METHANE} \qquad \begin{array}{c} H \\ | \\ H - C - H \\ | \\ H \end{array}$$

C stands for an atom of carbon

H stands for an atom of hydrogen

Carbon atoms can join each other to form a chain, the way people holding hands form a line. In a chain of carbon atoms, each carbon atom that is not at the end of the chain may use two of its bonds to hold on to the carbon atoms that are on either side of it. Then it has two bonds left with which it can hold on to two hydrogen atoms. Each carbon atom at the end of the chain may use only one bond to hold on to the carbon atom that is next to it. Then it has three bonds left with which it can hold on to three hydrogen atoms. The aliphatic compounds are all chains of carbon atoms that have other atoms attached to the sides and ends of the chain. The diagrams below show how chemists picture different kinds of chain-shaped molecules. Useful products are made from all of these compounds.

$$\begin{array}{cc} \overset{\displaystyle H}{\underset{\displaystyle H}{|}} \ \overset{\displaystyle H}{\underset{\displaystyle H}{|}} & \end{array}$$

H—C—C—H   H—C—C—C—H

ETHANE   PROPANE

In some molecules the carbon atoms form one or more closed rings instead of a long chain. Each ring has six carbon atoms. Each carbon atom in the ring is joined by one bond to the carbon atom on one side of it and by two bonds to the carbon atom on the other side of it. This leaves each carbon atom with one more bond with which it can hold on to another atom. Benzene is the simplest of these molecules with only one ring in the molecule. The diagram below shows how a chemist pictures the benzene ring.

H   BENZENE

Chemists sometimes use this diagram for a benzene molecule.

The chemical picture of coal is much more complicated than any of the pictures on page 38 or the pictures above. It looks like a lot of benzene rings placed side by side so that they look like chicken wire.

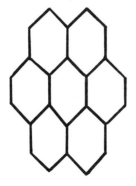

Diagram of part of a coal molecule

Getting at Coal's Hidden Riches

Chemicals made from coal are now being made in two different ways. One process makes the chemicals from the coke oven gases that are formed when coke is made. The other process makes the chemicals right from coal, without any in-between steps.

The *by-product coke oven* that is used now for coke-making does not waste the coke oven gas. The gas is piped away and most of the coal chemicals are taken out of it. The gas that is left is a lot like the gas made at gas-works. This gas may be used in two ways. It may be used for heating coke ovens. Or it may be used for making gasoline and other aliphatic compounds. In the United States most coal chemicals are made from coke oven gases. This process is called *carbonization* (CAR-bun-ih-ZAY-shun).

The process for making coal chemicals right from coal was invented about 50 years ago, at the same time that the by-product coke oven was first used. This process adds hydrogen to the carbon in the coal, so it is called *hydrogenation* (hy-drih-jih-NA-shun). A jet of hydrogen is blown through a heated mixture of iron and powdered coal. This produces a chemical mixture that can be separated into gasoline, Diesel oil, fuel oil and fuel gas.

Many new methods are being developed now for making gasoline from coal. One of them aims to make gasoline by combining coal with steam. The coal industry is also developing methods of coal *gasification* that change coal into methane and other gases to be sent to users through pipe lines.

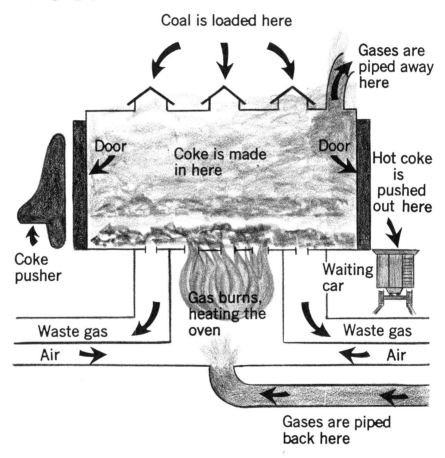

Coal is loaded here

Gases are piped away here

Door

Coke is made in here

Door

Hot coke is pushed out here

Coke pusher

Gas burns, heating the oven

Waiting car

Waste gas

Waste gas

Air

Air

Gases are piped back here

Schematic drawing of a by-product coke oven

The Problem of Dirty Air

When coal is burned, the gases produced go up into the air through chimneys and smokestacks. These gases may contain *pollutants*, solids and gases that dirty the air.

Black soot is formed when the burning coal does not get enough air to burn completely. The soot comes out of chimneys as black smoke. The formation of black smoke can be partly prevented by blowing a jet of air over the burning coal to make it burn better.

When coal burns, a dust called *fly ash* is formed. This dust, like soot, can be carried into the air by the gases that rise in a smokestack. Soot and fly ash falling out of the air settle on buildings, clothing, furniture, and people, and make them dirty. Fly ash and soot can be prevented from reaching the air if the gases produced by burning coal are passed through a dust collector before they go up the smokestack.

Coal contains some sulfur. When the coal is burned, the sulfur burns, too, and produces a gas called *sulfur dioxide*. When this gas rises into the air through smokestacks, it does a lot of damage to property and people. It spoils paint, rots cloth, and harms people's throats and lungs. Coal companies are now trying to find two separate ways of keeping sulfur dioxide out of the air. One way would be to crush the coal into a powder, and remove the sulfur from the coal before it is burned. The other way would be to remove the sulfur dioxide from the chimney gases after the coal is burned.

To clean up the air above them, many cities now have smoke control laws. These laws require that smoke be passed through a dust collector before it is released into the air. They also forbid the use of coal that has a lot of sulfur in it.

The city of Pittsburgh used to be called the "Smoky City" because of the large amount of smoke in its air. Now it has cleaner air because of its smoke control law. The pictures on page 44 show the same view of the city before and after the smoke control law went into effect.

A modern dust collector

The collector is made up of rows of tube-shaped glass fiber bags. Each bag is a filter.

1946
BEFORE

1956
AFTER

Coal versus Oil

Sixty years ago four-fifths of the energy used in the United States came from coal. In 1973 only one-sixth came from coal. Coal's share of the energy used has dropped partly because of the increased use of cars and trucks that burn gasoline and oil, and partly because oil and natural gas have taken the place of coal in the furnaces of many factories and electric power plants.

The use of more oil was possible as long as the oil industry found more oil and natural gas each year than was burned up that year. But the situation has changed. During the 1960's the United States used oil and gas faster than it found new supplies. As a result there is a growing shortage of oil and gas. In 1972 the United States had only enough oil and gas in the ground to last about 20 years.

However, there is no shortage of coal in the United States. Discovered coal reserves contain one and a half million million tons of coal, enough to last about two thousand years. For this reason, and because of the oil shortage, coal production will have to begin increasing sharply during the years 1975 to 1985. Coal is coming back to be used in two ways, as a fuel to be burned directly, and as a material from which oil and gas can be made.

Coal and the Future

During the next fifteen years the United States will need more and more energy. For every 25 units of energy used one year, 26 units will be needed the next year. The amount of energy used in 1985 will be double the amount used in 1970. The increased amount of energy used will come mainly from two sources, from nuclear power plants, and from increased use of coal and of oil and gas made from coal.*

Nuclear power plants produce energy by splitting the atom. By 1985 they will supply only a small amount of the energy needed. By the year 2000 they will supply about half the electricity used in the United States.

In 1973 the United States produced about 600 million tons of coal. By 1985 it should produce about four times as much to meet the growing need for energy.

Meanwhile new ways of producing energy are being studied. Scientists are looking for ways of releasing nuclear energy by fusion. They are exploring ways of using geothermal energy, or the heat of the earth. They are also trying to develop practical ways of catching and using the energy of sunlight. Once these new methods are perfected the supply of usable energy will be enough to last millions of years.

* For more information about nuclear power, see Atomic Energy, by Irving Adler, The John Day Company, 1971.

Index

About the Author

The *Reason Why* Books were initiated by Irving and Ruth Adler, who worked together to write the first thirty books in the series. Since his wife, Ruth, died in 1968, Irving Adler has continued the series.

Irving and Ruth Adler wrote jointly or separately eighty books about science and mathematics. Dr. Adler has been an instructor in mathematics at Columbia University and at Bennington College, and was formerly head of the mathematics department of a New York City high school. Ruth Adler taught mathematics, science, and art in schools in the New York area, and later also taught at Bennington. In addition to working with her husband writing *Reason Why* books, she drew the illustrations for most of them as well as for many other books written by him.

Books by Irving Adler alone and books by him in collaboration with Ruth Adler have been printed in 117 different foreign editions, in fifteen languages and in ten reprint editions.

PICTURE CREDITS

Pages 1 and 6 — Bureau of Mines, United States Department of the Interior
Pages 17 — After Agricola
Pages 24, 29, 31, 32 and 45 — National Coal Association
Pages 26 and 27 — Joy Manufacturing Company
Page 26 — Marion Power Shovel Co., a division of Universal Marion Corporation
Page 26 — Salem Tool Co. — Old Ben Coal Corp.
Page 27 — Joy Manufacturing Co. — Long-Airdox Co.
Page 35 — Baltimore and Ohio R.R.
Page 43 — The Pangborn Corp.
Page 44 — Allegheny Conference on Community Development
Pages 46 and 47 — General Electric